With love, FROM AUS

A COLLECTION OF STORIES FROM YOUR FRIENDS IN AUSTRALIA

HarperCollins*Publishers*

We acknowledge the Traditional Aboriginal and Torres Strait Islander Owners of the land, sea and waters of the Australian continent, and recognise their custodianship of culture and Country for over 60,000 years.

Aboriginal and Torres Strait Islander people are advised that this book may contain images of persons now deceased.

CONTENTS

FOREWORD

'AN EXHALATION. THAT'S THE ONLY WAY I CAN DESCRIBE IT.'

Laura Brown
Editor-in-chief, InStyle *magazine*

An exhalation. That's the only way I can describe it. When I head home to Australia, I finally stop holding my breath. Then, when I leave, I take another slow, deep inhalation and plunge, headlong, back into the world.

And that's when things were 'normal'. All of us have been holding our breath while the world works through the darkness, and Australians long to welcome the world's adventurers back to our shores. (Pretty sure our marsupials feel this way too – they live for attention).

As for me, I fantasise about what I'll do when I get off the plane, where I'll go, what I'll eat...who I'll hug. But mostly, of course, it's just being 'home' that I dream about. Landing at the airport to a broad, 'Howzit going?' from the customs officer. Coming out, dragging my bags, smelling coffee and toasted sandwiches. The weird, guttural sounds of birds (at least you think it's a bird?) in the eucalyptus trees. Getting in a taxi, opening the window and smelling the air. As we're fond of saying, the feeling is one of (please apply heavy Aussie accent here), 'swoyt reloyf'.

I'm honoured to write the forward to *With Love, From Aus* because Australia is an anchor. The patchwork of stories told here by some of our greatest talents and expats dance beautifully around that theme. The blessing and the curse of 'the land down under' is its distance from the world. As Australians, we hunger to be part of it all, to be 'international'. That's why we save our money, throw on that storied backpack and get on the plane. Most of us come home, enriched by the adventure but content to return. Some of us don't, scrambling hungrily to experience what we feel we didn't have.

But the longer we've been away, the more we appreciate and crave the things we so blithely cast aside: kangaroos, koalas, wombats, quokkas, cockatoos, gum trees, waratahs, jasmine, frangipanis. Red dirt. The sky that goes forever.

And while this book is about a state of mind, so much of what drives Australians – and attracts others to our shores – comes from nature, whether you're in the outback or a harbourside apartment. It comes from having space, for body and being. From freedom of movement and thought. From feeling safe. From having time. From falling down and getting up. From multiculturalism and mateship. And, of late, from simply taking care of each other during one of the greatest challenges in our communal lifetime.

They say Australians are down to earth, easygoing, up for it. They're right. We're really just happy to be there. I walk into a room full of 'my people', anywhere in the world, and I can feel my shoulders drop. There's an immediate familiarity, a lack of performance, a sense of the given. Leave us unsupervised for too long – and with a beverage or three – and we will break into insanely broad accents we've never even had. All the tension in your body disappears. Someone should bottle this feeling, because lord knows, we'd drink it.

'THIS BOOK IS ABOUT A STATE OF MIND.'

What makes Australia special, what governs it, is a simplicity. Being simple, to me, is the greatest compliment. To value the things that matter, to explore but to keep things close, to not get lost in the muck and the mire.

I think the more our stories are lived and shared, the better off we'd all be. Some might say that sounds arrogant, but Aussies don't do that. It's merely that deep breath that you let out and makes you stronger.

Sitting proudly, surrounded by sea, a hemisphere away, we send our love from Aus.

CHAPTER 1

Chris Hemsworth

SHOES OPTIONAL

Chris Hemsworth is one of the world's most sought-after actors.
When not starring in a Hollywood blockbuster, he can often be found
in Byron Bay on the northern coast of New South Wales, where he
and his actress wife, Elsa Pataky, are raising their three children.

'THERE IS SOMETHING ABOUT BEING FAR AWAY, DISCONNECTED FROM THE WORLD AND LIVING AMONG THE ELEMENTS THAT IS INCREDIBLY REFRESHING.'

Chris Hemsworth

We have a caravan that we love to take up and down the coast. My wife, Elsa, and I pack up the kids and head out to see new places. We are making an effort to give our kids similar experiences to what Elsa and I had growing up – to give them opportunities to adventure, explore and learn in nature.

For me, travelling and exploring corners of this country is all about being exposed to other ways of living. My parents definitely did their best to educate me and my two brothers, Liam and Luke, about different ways of life and different types of people and communities. Travelling and taking in the diverse, beautiful parts of this country really influenced and shaped who I am. It was a really important part of my childhood.

When you experience many cultures and places firsthand – when you're immersed in it – that's the best way to learn anything. So Elsa and I definitely want to give our three children, India Rose, Sasha and Tristan, as many experiences as possible. That then gives them the opportunity to decide who they're going to be and the type of people they're going to become, based on what they've seen.

Exploring new places encourages openness and acceptance of diversity. You get to see that we are all unique in a wonderful way.

I was fortunate that my parents not only took us kids travelling, but that they also gave us the most amazing experience when we moved as a family to live in the outback, in southern Arnhem Land.

Chris on the beach with family and friends

A young Chris and his mum, Leonie

A young Chris with his dad, Craig, and brother Luke

I was about three years old the first time we moved to Bulman. My earliest and most vivid memories of my childhood were formed in this very remote Aboriginal community about four and a half hours outside of Katherine in the Northern Territory.

In Bulman we lived on cattle stations, and at one point my parents ran a community resource centre. I remember not owning a pair of shoes because of how warm it was. Shoes were pretty much unnecessary up there.

I also remember the buffalo walking through the little community, a lot of snakes, crocodiles in the rivers, and feeling like life was just one big adventure. It was amazing.

The second time we went up north I was six or seven. My overwhelming memory is of the Aboriginal people who we lived with, worked with and went to school with. They were incredibly warm, open and fascinating. Being exposed to Aboriginal culture at a very young age was such a blessing. I love the First Nation people's strong connection to nature, and to the land. From living in Bulman, I developed a love of Aboriginal artwork, and learnt how they pass on their teachings and the stories of their history through art. It also literally illustrates their relationship to the land. My time in Bulman also allowed me to witness and learn about Aboriginal land management and practices. I loved the storytelling.

That outback experience was a real privilege – the older I get, the more I appreciate how valuable it was.

Elsa and I took our kids camping for the first time at Red Bluff in Western Australia. It was an incredibly remote desert space and to this day, the kids quite regularly bring up that camping trip and ask when we're going back there. I love being outdoors, and having sunset dinners with my family during that holiday was awesome.

There's something about being far away, disconnected from the world and living among the elements that is incredibly refreshing.

After a few years, my family moved to a completely different environment – to Phillip Island in Victoria. That's where I learnt to surf, spending more hours in the water than out. The water temperature down in southern parts of Australia can definitely be a bit on the cool side at times, but I love how rugged and raw the ocean is there. Some of my happiest memories are surfing at Phillip Island with my brothers and Dad and Mum. It's why living near the beach is very important to me now.

'THAT OUTBACK EXPERIENCE WAS A REAL PRIVILEGE.'

Another special place in my childhood is Mallacoota. I remember spending nearly all my childhood summers in that very small country surf town on the Victorian coastline. Mum had been camping there ever since she was a little girl, with my grandparents, and then we started going there as kids, as a family.

For two weeks every year just after Christmas we'd set up our tents, and then it would be surf-fish-eat-sleep, all in that little pattern, and nothing else. There was fantastic surf there, and I remember having some wonderful friends that I'd only see once a year. We'd fall back into our summer routine – not much changed from year to year in Mallacoota.

Chris with a quokka at Rottnest Island, Western Australia

'THE QUALITY OF LIFE IN BYRON BAY IS SECOND TO NONE.'

We chose to live in Byron rather than Los Angeles so we could be closer to nature, water, the bush. So we could have a quieter life. I really wanted our kids to grow up around the stunning landscapes I had as a kid.

When I was living in Los Angeles, I'd be constantly reminded about the film industry and everyone you meet is somehow involved. So, coming back here and being around people in different professions and spending my time on horses and motorbikes, or wandering barefoot through the produce markets is a dream come true.

It wasn't a simple decision to make. Elsa is from Spain so we were facing a pretty tricky challenge of figuring out where we were going to live and raise our kids. We were originally living in America together, then our daughter was born in the UK, and the boys were born in America. We really did have a long hard think about a lot of different places. The first couple of times I brought Elsa here to Australia, she felt completely at ease – she loved the environment, and she's a very sporty, outdoors person, so it ticked all the boxes for her sense of adventure and her need to be deeply connected with nature.

I think Australians and Spaniards share a similar mindset; Spanish people love to socialise and get together and have big dinners and barbeques and so on. They share our communal need to have a good time.

I have to travel for work but when I return to Australia, I find it's incredibly grounding just setting foot back in this country. It's an instant reset when I step off the plane and I come back and have a surf. No matter what emotional state I'm in, or whether I'm jet lagged, the stress I might have felt with work all seems to just dissipate when I get home.

It's almost like nature speaks the language of 'no worries' – it seems to be our country itself speaking.

As a family, we're immediately drawn to the outdoors and have built our lifestyle in and around nature.

We can't keep the kids out of the water and that's where we usually venture when we have time away from work. They have that same sort of obsession with the ocean and with water as Elsa and I do.

A few years back, we went up to the Great Barrier Reef. My boys were a bit young to snorkel, but my daughter loved it. One of the most special times for me was seeing her wide-eyed fascination with the marine life that was going on under the surface. It was pretty incredible to watch.

I went scuba diving for the first time there which was amazing. The diversity of sea life and colours is unlike anything I've ever seen. It's like visiting another planet. Flying over the reef and seeing the changing blues and greens was also incredible. Such intense colours and contrast to the white sand of the beaches.

On that trip we also had an afternoon at Whitehaven Beach which was absolutely stunning. The most pristine white sand, crystal clear water. The perfect spot to just unwind surrounded by the reef. The next day we took the kids for a picnic and a bit of beach cricket on Langford Island, just off Hayman Island. The kids loved running along the sand and playing in the shallows.

Another memorable trip we did as a family was seeing Uluru for the first time. We had the very special experience of meeting with Sammy Wilson, a local Anangu traditional owner. Listening to the Indigenous people speaking about the cultural and spiritual significance of Uluru was fascinating and inspiring. The kids loved running around the base of the rock and exploring all the little caves and trails. And there was an art installation on called Field of Light, and the colours at sunrise were amazing.

'WE HAVE BUILT OUR LIFESTYLE IN AND AROUND NATURE.'

I travel all over the world for my job and have been fortunate enough to visit some beautiful corners of this earth, but I wouldn't want to live anywhere else.

The natural beauty of Australia is what always surprises me. From the Red Centre and Uluru with their rich desert landscapes, to the stunning gorges and remote waterholes of the Kimberley, and some of the world's most beautiful and pristine coastlines. There are places where the red dirt meets crystal clear turquoise water, and you can go days exploring the coast without seeing anyone else.

Here in Australia, the most common phrases you're going to hear are 'No worries, mate', or 'She'll be right, mate', or 'Don't worry about it' – and I feel our environment here impresses that upon you as well.

That's why we choose to live here. In my opinion, Australia has it all.

Chris with his son Sasha

'Like many Aussies, growing up on the coast instilled a deep respect for the environment, our oceans, and marine life. I always felt a profound responsibility to preserve this beauty for generations to come.'

Pete Ceglinski

**Co-founder and CEO,
Seabin Project**

CHAPTER 2

Adam Hills
NO
WORRIES

*Adam Hills is one of Australia's most recognised comedians,
celebrated for his unique take on the late-night talk show,
Adam Hills Tonight, and the iconic music quiz show* Spicks and Specks.
*A five-time Gold Logie nominee for Most Popular Personality on
Australian Television, Adam has taken the UK by storm as the host
of the multi-award-winning talk show* The Last Leg *on Channel 4.*

'TWO WORDS THAT PERFECTLY SUM UP AN ATTITUDE, A STATE OF MIND, AND AN OUTLOOK ON LIFE.'

Adam Hills

There is a scene in the movie *The Lion King*. You know the one. It's where Timon (the meerkat) and Pumbaa (the warthog) try to explain to young lion Simba the meaning of 'hakuna matata'.

They (and the songwriters) clearly racked their brains to find a universally understood way to describe the tricky Swahili mantra, and eventually settled on a phrase that everybody in the world could easily digest. Two words that perfectly sum up an attitude, a state of mind, and an outlook on life.

'It means "no worries".'

And suddenly everyone's on board.

Whether you're a furry critter on the African savannah, or an American audience member in a Midwest cinema, you know what 'no worries' means, and you know where it comes from.

It means 'Relax, don't stress, just take it easy for a while' and it comes from the Land Down Under.

The 'no worries' attitude is as much a part of Australian life as Uluru, snakes and suntan cream. Although I'd argue that 'no worries' came about *because* of Uluru, snakes and suntan cream.

Let's work backwards, and start with suntan cream.

Put simply – it's too hot to worry.

When I first started performing stand-up comedy in Britain, I was asked why there aren't more angry Australian comedians. I replied that it's pretty hard to get wound up about the state of the world when you've spent all day on a beach.

The general Aussie climate seems to hit that sweet spot of humidity, heat and proximity to water that engenders a feeling of relaxation. I mean, no one has ever submerged themselves in a warm bath in order to fire themselves up.

Obviously there are some exceptions to the rule, like the tropics for instance, where the heat and moisture combine to send some people slightly off kilter. Even then, though, we're too laidback to give it a multisyllabic medical description, instead opting for the term 'gone troppo'.

Secondly the snakes. And the spiders, and jellyfish, and some octopi. Yes they exist, but the likelihood of ever coming across one is pretty slim. So why worry about it?

It's a state of mind illustrated by a recent TV show I filmed called *The Last Leg Down Under*. We were in Darwin, picking up branches from the side of the road, when my English co-host asked our Aussie guide, 'Could there be a spider under this?'

'RELAX, DON'T STRESS, JUST TAKE IT EASY FOR A WHILE.'

The reply was: 'There could be. But there probably won't be.'

See what I mean?

There's no point stressing about something that has a very small chance of happening. If we were in any way worried about creepy-crawlies, our national dress wouldn't be a pair of flip-flops.

Finally, the natural beauty of Australia. When faced with the stunning vista of Sydney Harbour, the majesty of Uluru, the serenity of Broome, the spectacle of the Great Ocean Road – it's kinda hard not to feel in awe. Like you're a small part of something much greater and more powerful than yourself.

That sense of contemplation tends to lead to a sense of relaxation. And you very rarely see a stressed-out Buddhist.

Ironically, I once read that the first English people to set eyes on Aboriginal people in and around Sydney Harbour were critical of their lifestyle. They were apparently appalled that the women sat around giggling on the beach, while the men lay languidly in the shade.

Two hundred-odd years later, we encouraged British tourists to visit the same shores, so that they could spend their time giggling on beaches or lying around languidly in the shade.

Turns out the original inhabitants of Australia were practising the 'no worries' mantra, well before white people even set eyes on the country.

Because that's what the place does to you.

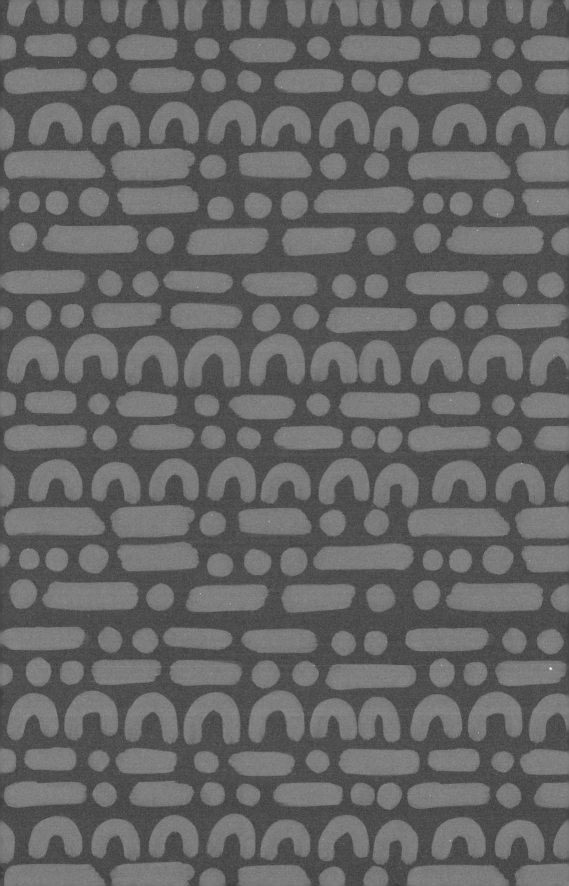

'I'm privileged to live and work on the Great Barrier Reef, one of the most beautiful and wild places on the planet. Every moment spent on the Reef is a powerful inspiration to do everything we can to protect our precious environment.'

Andy Ridley

Co-founder, Earth Hour and CEO, Citizens of the Great Barrier Reef

CHAPTER 3

Mick Fanning

GET OFF THE BEATEN TRACK

*Mick Fanning is one of the world's greatest surfing heroes,
with an impressive competitive record that includes three world titles.
The man they called White Lightning retired in 2018
after a 16-year pro-surfing career.*

'AS SURFERS WE'RE ALWAYS TRYING TO FIND THE MOST AMAZING WAVES WITH NO ONE ELSE AROUND. A LOT OF THE TIME THAT MEANS YOU JUST FOLLOW YOUR OWN PATH...'

Mick Fanning

I was born in the western suburbs of Sydney in a town called Penrith. The beach was a two-hour drive away. Our mum would load us into her little red bomb, the radio blasting with old rock songs, and drive us down the coast.

We didn't have much but we didn't need much – we had each other and that was plenty.

I'm the youngest of five. With three older brothers, competition was a part of life when we were growing up. We battled for everything: food, toys and eventually waves. I think that's where my competitive nature comes from.

My three big brothers started surfing and, as annoying younger siblings tend to do, I followed them. It wasn't until we moved to Coffs Harbour when I was three that the five of us started doing little adventures to the beach on a daily basis.

In Coffs, we lived just two blocks from the beach. We'd walk out the house, across the footy field, walking in a line, just like little ants (with surfboards under our arms), then through the bush and onto the beach.

By the time I was five, I was out on the big waves alongside my brothers. I would trust the three of them to put me into the right situations. But they would pretty much just push me out the back of the waves. It was like, 'Sink or swim, buddy.'

Mick Fanning wins the final of the JBay Open, 2016

They pushed me to trust myself, but at the same time they probably put me in danger a little bit. I remember as a five-year-old getting sucked out in a vicious rip and my mum had to come and save me. She was pretty frightened. But it was all part of a very adventurous childhood, I guess.

Life was great and got even better when Mum took a job on the Gold Coast. We moved up there, and I started competing in junior events and getting results. Pretty soon sponsorship contracts began coming my way and becoming a pro surfer became the dream and then a reality.

I reckon a strong sense of adventure shaped my career. As surfers we're always trying to find the most amazing waves with no one else around. A lot of the time that means you just follow your own path, looking for waves that not necessarily everyone's going to find.

Everyone might be turning right and you go, 'Alright, I'm going to turn left and see what's down this street.' That's an attitude that is definitely in a lot of surfers' DNA, trying to find waves without another soul around.

That's something great about Australia, that you can head down to places on our coastline, find a little beach and be completely by yourself. I feel that's something really special about this country.

I do think Australians have a boundless sense of spirit when it comes to adventure and persistence. We don't put limits on ourselves. When it comes to us as a sporting nation, I think we sort of see ourselves as underdogs and that's where we get our fighting spirit from.

We've gone into international contests underestimated, under-resourced, and yet we end up winning the title or taking the trophy. It's a huge achievement especially when we don't have a massive population like, say, America or Europe.

'AUSTRALIANS HAVE A BOUNDLESS SENSE OF SPIRIT.'

Early in my career, I always felt like I was a bit of an underdog and that's why I always tried to use all my strength and prove people wrong.

Some of the most adventurous Australians I know are athletes. You only have to look at someone like dual-Olympian turned endurance athlete Courtney Atkinson, who loves to trail-run through the most incredible landscapes. He does these crazy running adventures around Australia. One of them was to race over the best eight running trails in Australia, in just seven days. One for each state and territory in the country.

He ran amazing trails through Kings Canyon, Wilpena Pound, Wineglass Bay in Tassie, the Twelve Apostles in Victoria and Mount Kosciuszko, our highest peak.

But Courtney isn't alone. We've got skiers, dirt-bikers – there are too many to name. I think the reason these athletes do well in their field on the world stage comes back to our adventurous spirit as a nation.

'WE'RE PRETTY ADVENTUROUS AS A NATION. WHEN IT COMES TO HOLIDAYING WE'RE HAPPY TO GO AND TRY SOMETHING NEW, TO EXPLORE NEW PLACES.'

Sunday 19 July 2015 is a day I will never forget. I woke up feeling great. I was in South Africa competing in the J-Bay Open, the sixth event on the World Surf League Championship Tour. I was in the final against a really close mate, Julian Wilson. The winner of the event would take the ratings lead in the world title race, and I really felt like I was on my way to victory that day.

Around four minutes into the final, things got interesting when a great white shark appeared. Things happened so fast.

I punched and kicked out at the shark, trying to get away. I thought I was going to die. I guess everyone watching on from the beach that day, and on the live broadcast all over the world, thought the exact same thing.

I started swimming away, and all of a sudden the jetskis were there to help me out of the water. Julian, who had paddled towards me – and the shark – also helped me.

I'll never forget his valour that day and in the days that followed. It altered the course of my life, giving me perspective I'd never had before.

That incident at J-Bay wasn't a moment that changed my life. It was an experience that encouraged me to appreciate people around me and the things I did in life a little bit more.

It was a reminder to take nothing for granted. I make sure that if I'm engaging with someone, I properly engage with them. I make sure if I give a hug, if it's a close friend, make sure they feel it.

In a way that experience kind of gave me courage to go and try something new.

I was so caught up in this whole competition world, and then at the end of that year I was just mentally and physically exhausted so that I had to take some time off. I just tried to take a different path after that. It opened my eyes to the things that I enjoyed more, rather than competing day in, day out. In April 2018 I retired, I was done.

Retirement gave me the courage to try something new and to also back myself. And then also just be on my time really. I think when you're competing, you're always running to someone else's schedule and now for me it's – yeah, if I want to go on an adventure then I want to be able to just drop everything and leave. Whereas in the past I've had to plan it out a year in advance. So now it's being on *my* time and if that sense of adventure wants to come up then I'm not scared to just go and do it.

Don't get me wrong, going around the world and travelling to all these amazing places each and every year was truly amazing. But it got to a point where I wanted to go and explore different places that weren't on the professional surfing tour, including my own backyard.

A pretty awesome aspect of this country is being able to hit the road for a few hours or more and go and explore somewhere new. It's great that you can rock up with no expectations and discover a whole new part of the country you've never seen before.

As Australians we're not scared to just go on an adventure to find something that may or may not make us happy. We know how big the world is and we just want to go and explore everything. It's a pretty typical thing for kids to finish school or university and then just jump on a plane and travel the globe for two, three years.

We're pretty adventurous as a nation. When it comes to holidaying we're happy to go and try something new, to explore new places.

But there are plenty of places to check out in our own backyard. And in different ways too. Like, if you want to go and live it right up there are amazing and cool hotels in cities like Brisbane, Sydney and Perth.

Or you can go off the beaten path, get off the grid and go camping – that's what I'm into at the moment. I like going camping with mates: Moreton Island is one of my favourites. It's a beautiful, unspoilt paradise where you can just go and get away from civilisation a bit and chill out.

On Moreton Island there are massive sand dunes, glassy lakes, rocky outcrops, wild forests, beautiful beaches and a lonely lighthouse. Moreton is almost completely sand with no roads, so a four-wheel drive car is needed if you are going further than walking distance from the ferry landing points.

It's one place I have visited often since I stopped surfing professionally. Now I have more time on my hands, I have a bucket list of where I would like to go, starting at the Great Australian Bight then heading up through the Kimberley. I've never been up Darwin way. They're probably the three biggest ones at the moment I would like to head to.

I found my sense of adventure on the waves, and I still want to see what else is out there and meet new characters. To not have everything so easy. To get out of my comfort zone a little bit – that's where I'm at today.

Mick Fanning strolls through Moreton Island

CHAPTER 4

Mike Cannon-Brookes
BOUNDLESS OPTIMISM

Mike Cannon-Brookes is the Co-founder and Co-CEO of Atlassian, based in Sydney. He and Scott Farquhar started the company soon after graduating from college in 2002. Atlassian's team collaboration software is used by more than 200,000 customers around the world, including NASA, Tesla and Netflix. Cannon-Brookes has been a vocal advocate for action on climate change and the adoption of renewable energy in Australia.

'WE ARE THE SUNNIEST COUNTRY ON EARTH OUTSIDE OF THE SUB-SAHARA ... WE'RE ALSO ONE OF THE WINDIEST. BUT OUR RESOURCES ARE NOT JUST PHYSICAL THINGS, THEY'RE AS MUCH ABOUT PEOPLE AS THEY ARE WIND AND SUN.'

Mike Cannon-Brookes

As Australians we are an optimistic bunch. We have built a country in a place where building isn't easy and conditions can be harsh. But as a nation, we've totally smashed it.

We figured things out from being on the land, from fighting through world wars, from playing our part in the global economy and from our Indigenous heritage stretching back tens of thousands of years.

We are resourceful people, we're survivors. We've had to be brave. We've faced obstacles with energy and courage. Today we're bringing those characteristics to almost every industry.

When Scott and I started our software company, Atlassian, we did it on a credit card, eating two-minute noodles, and coding through the night. When it was cold, we'd run our fingers under the hot water tap so we could keep working. It was tough! But we wanted to start something new. We didn't want to go and work for some-one else, wearing a suit to the office every day. We had an idea, we wanted to make it work and we wanted to build it here in Australia.

This sort of boundless optimism is quintessentially Aussie. And it's not confined to the world Scott and I hang out in. Look to Hollywood – there are many Australian actors who have conquered the world stage. And that's because they are Australians – they arrived in Los Angeles optimistic and resourceful.

Manufactured in Adelaide, South Australia, the Hills hoist is just
one of the everyday innovations invented Down Under

Head 500 kilometres north of Hollywood to Silicon Valley and you will find Australians have a pretty good reputation there too. In tech we've got a great history, no matter how far you go back. We are seen as having a highly knowledgeable population. Certainly in the last 10 years our reputation has been excellent.

The tyranny of distance doesn't affect tech as much as it does other industries. It's much harder when you have to build physical things and ship them around the world. But tech is weightless. We can build and grow profitable global businesses.

We're not into froth-and-bubbles ideas that might disappear.

'WHEN IT COMES TO INNOVATION, AUSTRALIA PUNCHES ABOVE ITS WEIGHT.'

We invented wi-fi – we always tell people that. We've invented a wide range of things: the black box flight recorder, the pacemaker, the ultrasound, the Hills hoist, the flushing toilet, the lawnmower and Vegemite.

With innovations like the cochlear bionic ear or the Gardasil vaccine, we've built incredible global companies from Australia. If we'd sold Atlassian 15 years ago and then gone to work somewhere in California, we would have done the innovation but not the commercialisation.

I think we are getting better at commercialising our ideas and products. The bottom line is: we *have* to be innovative as a country. It comes back to our DNA and our history of thinking, *We're on the far side of the planet, surviving in a pretty harsh land, so we've just got to make our own stuff.* We are irrepressible optimists and we find solutions. Our values shape our thinking – we build trust, we are resourceful and we are creative.

We are always looking for new ways to improve the way things are done. For example, the Hills hoist was developed in Adelaide, South Australia, by World War II veteran Lance Hill in 1945. Lance Hill got home from the war and realised his backyard was getting crowded, so he designed and built a rotary clothesline from some old pipe.

Back then you didn't go to Bunnings to get something, you had to make it.

We're seen as very practical in that we make practical stuff that solves real people's problems. We know we're going to figure it out. This applies to the tech industry too.

When it comes to innovation, Australia punches above its weight. I'm excited by the next wave of innovation, especially in the world of energy. Australia could be a renewable energy superpower. We've just got to have the vision and insight to go after it.

I'm often asked about my views on energy and the climate emergency that confronts us. It's an issue that many of our employees at Atlassian care about. And it's the reason that Atlassian is going 100 per cent renewable by 2025. Loads of other big companies are doing the same.

As a nation, I hope Australia ends up as the world's superpower in renewable energy. We have a crazy amount of natural energy resources. It's both our blessing and our curse.

We are the sunniest country on Earth outside of the sub-Sahara and we are also one of the windiest countries on Earth. But our resources are not just rocks and physical things, they're as much about people as they are wind and sun.

We should export those resources.

We live next to three billion people in Asia who really need the energy our natural resources give us every day. It's actually no different conceptually to digging up iron ore and shipping steel to China because they're building city after city after city – it's just we have to conceptualise that.

Getting to 200 per cent renewable energy is about saying we're going to not only fill our own consumption, but we're going to export what's left over. Besides being aspirational, that also turns out to be an incredibly smart economic move for the country.

Australians have been exporting stuff for hundreds of years. It's a talent of ours. We are a nation that's built to export. We've known this since the wool industry started back in 1797 and then boomed in the 1880s.

When we discovered wool, we finally had a good product to send overseas. It was something we could make a lot of. It was light enough that you could put it on a wooden boat, and would not degrade during the three or four months it took to get to England and sell it.

Before 1840, Australia was producing more than two million kilos of wool each year. That's where the saying emerged that 'Australia was built on a sheep's back'.

'WE HAVE TO BE INNOVATIVE AS A COUNTRY.'

Fast-forward almost 200 years, and today tech companies are taking up the export mantle.

If you look at all the big tech companies in Australia, we export 95 per cent of our software overseas. We are manufacturers, we build it; then we're an exporter, we send it overseas. We sell software all over the world.

In energy, it's no different. We naturally have an exporting mindset and we have to adapt. The exporting market is already there.

Australians don't back down. We want to solve global challenges, and a lot of us are out there trying to do just that. We're very close to the land. It's a big part of our mental history as a country. Whether you think of Bondi Beach, or the Whitsundays, or Uluru, or the bush or the gum trees, we have a very big national sense of this land; it's very important to who we are.

In fact, it's part of our DNA. Here we are on the far side of the planet, surviving and thriving.

That's the sort of mindset we try to maintain every day. We may have started small, but today Australian ingenuity has travelled far and wide. And we are building the next generation of big new ideas. That's boundless optimism.

'Australia is a place of inspiring people, and a place that has allowed me to undertake my most important research into some of the world's most pressing waste and sustainability challenges.'

Prof. Veena Sahajwalla

ARC Laureate
UNSW SMaRT Centre Director,
SMaRT@UNSW

CAPE LEVEQUE, WESTERN AUSTRALIA

At the most northern tip of the Dampier Peninsula lies 240 kilometres of pristine, sandy beaches.
It's loved by all visitors – wild turtles, soaring seabirds, whales and their newborns.

TARYL BUKULATJPI, ARNHEM LAND, NORTHERN TERRITORY

'When you're on country with an Aboriginal person, you realise how little you
know and how magnificent and beautiful this culture is here.' – *Ben Shewry*

LUCKY BAY, WESTERN AUSTRALIA

ECHIDNA ON THREE CAPES TRACK, TASMANIA

Hiking the 46 kilometres of trails along the dramatic Tasman Peninsula is always
better with a mate. Especially when that mate's a prickly little echidna.

KANGAROOS AT LUCKY BAY, WESTERN AUSTRALIA

'Australian wildlife is incredibly unique and like many people who
visit Australia, having a wildlife experience was my main motivation
to travel here back in 1991.' – *Terri Irwin*

BAIRD BAY, SOUTH AUSTRALIA

Australian sea lions are extremely sociable creatures who constantly call for each other.
It's no surprise they're not one bit shy when it comes to showing off their water acrobatics.

GLOW WORM TUNNEL, WOLLEMI NATIONAL PARK, NEW SOUTH WALES

'Exploring new places encourages openness and acceptance of diversity.
You get to see that we are all unique in a wonderful way.' – *Chris Hemsworth*

ULURU-KATA TJUTA NATIONAL PARK, NORTHERN TERRITORY

BLUE MOUNTAINS NATIONAL PARK, NEW SOUTH WALES

'We have a very big national sense of this land, it's very important to who we are.
In fact, it's part of our DNA.' – *Mike Cannon-Brookes*

TWELVE APOSTLES, GREAT OCEAN ROAD, VICTORIA

The jewel in the crown of the Great Ocean Road, the Twelve Apostles are
unforgettable limestone monuments. These amazing formations are stunning
at all times but become all the more beautiful in the golden hour.

WILD SWAN RESTAURANT, MANDOON ESTATE, SWAN VALLEY, WESTERN AUSTRALIA

Sometimes the perfect way to end (or start) a meal is with dessert. In Australia,
we combine the finest local produce – pears, honey, hazelnuts – whatever is fresh
and in season, with classic techniques to create the most exquisite treats.

FERMENTING PROCESS AT D'ARENBERG, MCLAREN VALE, SOUTH AUSTRALIA

Best known for its shiraz, McLaren Vale is the home for world-class winemakers
who still use timeless techniques, like basket-pressing and foot-treading.

WAVE ROCK, HYDEN, WESTERN AUSTRALIA

Wave Rock is a granite cliff that rises 15 metres from the outback plain.
Millions of years of erosion have resulted in a formation that resembles
a breaking wave, unlike any you'll see at sea.

MACKAY CORAL CAY, QUEENSLAND

'It's great that you can rock up with no expectations and discover a whole
new part of the country you've never seen before.' – *Mick Fanning*

FLORIADE, CANBERRA, AUSTRALIAN CAPITAL TERRITORY

Floriade is the largest flower festival in the Southern Hemisphere. Millions of technicoloured blooms – tulips, pansies, poppies, violets, ranunculus, hyacinths, irises, daisies, bellis – welcome visitors, including a fair few peckish cockatoos.

GREAT BARRIER REEF, QUEENSLAND

'The diversity of sea life and colours is unlike anything I've ever seen.
It's like visiting another planet.' – *Chris Hemsworth*

'Living in this exquisite, abundant country, Australia, I have an overwhelming sense of joy as to my good fortune. This led me to ask what more I could do for others.'

Ronni Kahn

Founder and CEO,
OzHarvest

CHAPTER 5

Warwick Thornton

HAVE A STORY TO TELL

Warwick Thornton is an Indigenous Australian cinematographer and director. His debut feature film, Samson & Delilah (2009), won the Caméra d'Or at the Cannes Film Festival.

'YOU KNOW, 50,000 YEARS AGO MY GREAT-GREAT-GREAT-GREAT-GREAT-GREAT-GRANDMOTHER WOULD'VE SAT AROUND A FIRE AND TOLD A STORY... TODAY I'M DOING THE SAME THING, JUST WITH A DIFFERENT MEDIUM.'

Warwick Thornton

You know, I'm Kaytej, I'm from a very, very small town in the centre of Australia about 300 kilometres from Alice Springs, one of the most incredibly powerful, beautiful places.

In the 70s when I was a kid, I had very limited access to any form of story whether it was music, or cinema. We had a drive-in theatre and one called the walk-in, but they were both outdoor cinemas. It was incredibly hot in Alice so obviously they only worked at night, you couldn't watch movies during the day.

You'd hear about films or you'd read about them in magazines, and then five years later the film would appear in Alice. It took that long. By the time we saw them, prints would be ripped to shreds – scratches and big chunks taken out from bad projectionists around the world – but you took what you were given in a way. You didn't have a say in what kind of cinema you watched – we got really basic Hollywood popcorn cinema, like *Jaws* and *Star Wars*.

The most exciting thing happened when VHS – video cassettes – came along, because suddenly a video shop opened up in Alice. There was this room in town that held a thousand movies.

That's when I started to create my own path in what I watched. Now there was a whole wall of Australian films, a whole back catalogue of the birth of Australian cinema. I watched the amazing *Breaker Morant* and *Mad Max* and all those kind of films. In the beginning I hired a movie every night and I would re-watch them too. I would desperately wait for new titles to come in.

The VHS changed me. In a strange way, it gave me a kind of a conscience about storytelling.

Ultimately, I got into film to get out of Alice. I loved Alice – its cycles, its beer, blokes and barbeques, its wonderful culture, so many tribes on Arrernte land. I just thought there's got to be more ...

'There's the stories like songlines; the concept of traditional
storytelling with song and travelling. Using the song as a map.'

We come from an oral history. Our knowledge is actually power, where we come from. The hierarchy, if there is a hierarchy in the tribe, is because of knowledge, and knowledge comes with age. So that's how we work. Memory and story are actually a currency, in a way. Your memory is the most important thing that you can actually have.

There's the stories like songlines; the concept of traditional storytelling with song and travelling. Using the song as a map. This isn't necessarily entertainment where we all sit around and have a good dance – the corroboree it's called in some places. It's not like going to a disco.

It's about actually rebuilding and creating a map. Those songlines are so incredibly important for survival because in the desert, where I come from, waterholes dry up and then there's water underground but it only comes out in certain places.

Those songlines are designed to tell you, say, where the water is or at this time of the year these plants are fruiting in this valley. How to survive in the desert is actually a song, and that is dangerously important, because it's about survival. You can't forgot that song.

It's kind of like a supermarket map and it's in your brain and it comes with a song. That's how important storytelling and song is to Indigenous people.

'I ALWAYS SAY, WHEN YOU LOOK INTO A FIRE OUT IN THE SCRUB, THIS IS BUSH TELEVISION.'

Those songs and that dance around that fire – there's light involved, there's sound involved, just the same as cinema or in a strange way now, television. What we own and technology keep changing, but the concept of storytelling doesn't. I firmly believe that. They reinvent the technology but they're not reinventing the concept of storytelling. And you know, 50,000 years ago my great-great-great-great-great-great-grandmother would've sat around a fire and told a story to the children – and today I'm doing the same thing, just with a different medium.

We're still passing those stories down orally. But now that we've got the film camera, or the radio mic, or the guitar, we're turning it into other forms of storytelling, and we're embracing it like you would for the first time, and that's important for us.

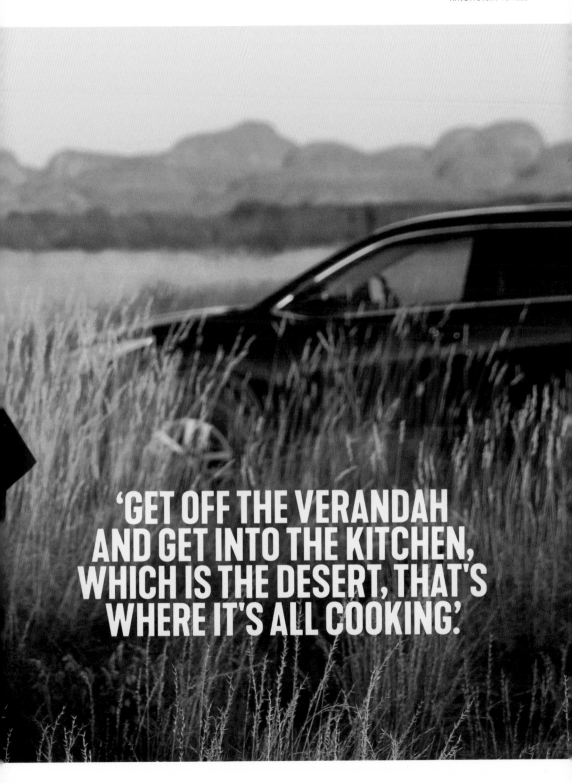

'GET OFF THE VERANDAH
AND GET INTO THE KITCHEN,
WHICH IS THE DESERT, THAT'S
WHERE IT'S ALL COOKING'.

I am not big on answers and a storybook ending. I want to create questions because the answer is in the person watching the film. So if I make a movie, that movie goes into cinemas, and I give people these stories that they've never seen before, then they become stronger human beings because they have more knowledge.

My films are dark, but they're completely truthful. I don't like to use director tricks to emotionally blackmail audiences. I don't want to put music in just so 'you have to feel sad now because it's a sad scene'. You make your own mind up. You're intelligent.

Before we started *Sweet Country* I said to my son River, 'Well, we need a second unit director, DOP, and I want you to do that.' And it shocked him more than anything, because it's a big movie but I thought he was ready.

We'd set up two shoots in a way at dusk, so we'd do two different scenes at the same time when the light's really, really nice, in that beautiful Australian twilight. He'd set off and he'd have three pages of the whole scene to do, and he'd come back with the most beautiful footage, and the most beautiful settings, incredibly well directed, composed, incredibly well shot, so that we can actually edit the scene.

He delivered shots better than mine, he'd worked so incredibly hard. Suddenly I'm second fiddle to my son – that was a really powerful moment.

'WE'RE AN AWESOME COUNTRY AND WE HAVE AN AWESOME STORY TO TELL.'

We will always have a voice, we'll always have our own stories that are about us as a country and not about us conforming to another country's point of view on us. We should be pleasing ourselves and empowering ourselves, not trying to please other countries in that way.

I don't want to sound nationalistic, it's more about this: we're an awesome country and we have an awesome story to tell.

Warwick and his son Dylan River

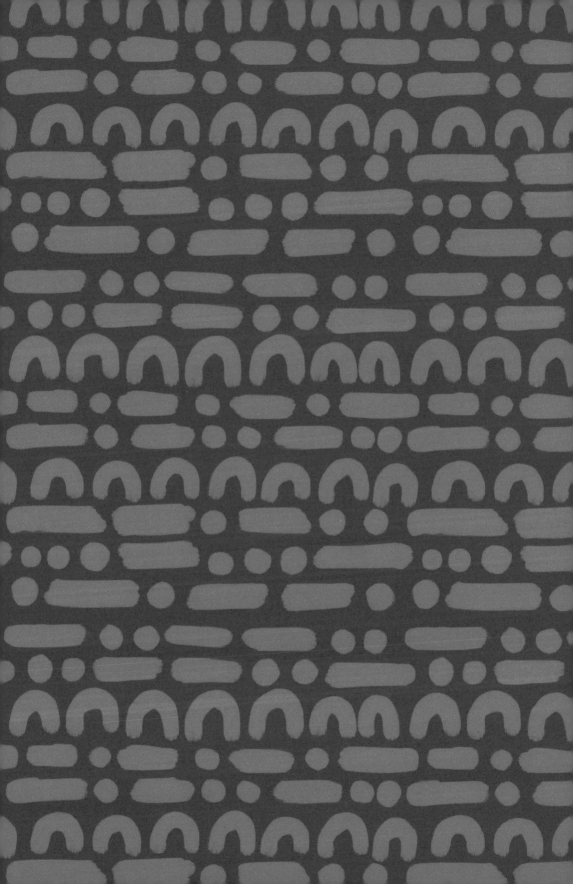

'The world's oldest living culture combined with cultures from across the globe makes Australia such a special and innovative place, sparking unprecedented innovation. I feel blessed to be immersed in it.'

Joost Bakker

Australian entrepreneur and eco-trailblazer

CHAPTER 6

Ben Shewry

A STRANGER IS A MATE YOU HAVEN'T MET YET

Ben Shewry is the chef and owner of Attica, one of Australia's and the world's best restaurants. His focus is on Australian native produce, from murnong to bunya nuts, and what it means to be an Australian restaurant.

'I LEARNT A LOT ABOUT KINDNESS IN AUSTRALIA. I FEEL LIKE PEOPLE WILL BE THERE ANY TIME I NEED HELP, THAT MY FRIENDS WILL BE THERE.'

Ben Shewry

I moved to Australia on 5 November 2002 when I was twenty-five years old. I had $500 in my pocket. That's all I had. I came to Melbourne to learn.

When I arrived, I felt incredibly accepted. Of course, the New Zealand jokes came thick and fast, but you've got to have a thick skin, you know? And it was all well-intentioned. There's a camaraderie – they're not saying, 'We don't like you'; they're saying, 'We do like you because we're hanging shit on you.'

I felt immediately welcome here, in this place, Melbourne, in this country, Australia. I had travelled the world and never really felt that before. Australia became home.

I remember this one hot December day just after arriving. It was 40-something degrees and I had never experienced such brutal heat in my life. I was really suffering. Where I'm from, it's hot if it gets above 25 degrees. I went down to Black Rock Beach, and it felt as if there were 3000 people in the water around me.

There's no surf at Black Rock. It's a bayside beach and I was sitting in the water amongst all these strangers. They were talking in every direction and were sounding like a giant flock of cockatoos: 'Hey, hi, how you are going?'; 'Hello, how's your day?'

There were groups of friends but also strangers chatting to strangers, and I just was blown away by the social dynamics and the 'we're all in this together' attitude. I think there's something in the 'If you're friendly, you're fine by me' approach that underpins society here. I found that I was accepted quickly because I was interested in others. So many of us had recently arrived and there wasn't the cliquishness of the community I'd come from.

Top: Noel and Trish Butler; Ben with Bruce Pascoe in Gipsy Point, Victoria
Bottom: Ben with Ash and Gary McBean in Southbank, Victoria; Ben and Gary McBean

It was an amazing scene down at the beach that day. It was a huge realisation that wow, this is really a different country to any other country that I've been in, including my home, New Zealand.

I saw openness and inclusiveness. I experienced people of all colours, nationalities, religions and orientations in the water together.

There are people I've met in Australia who have supported me and led me – a curious migrant – down a different path in the most beautiful and sensitive way. Being friends with them has changed my life.

I have an interest in native ingredients so when I came to Australia, I wanted to learn more about the First Nations people here. Aboriginal and Torres-Strait Islander people have a direct connection to the land and the country and an incredible history that goes back thousands and thousands of years. That's fascinating to me and I think our nation should learn about and collectively cherish it.

There are many who contribute to my ongoing education and help me to understand and celebrate this country, but two people stand out. Aboriginal elders Uncle Bruce Pascoe and Uncle Noel Butler are my window into First Nations culture. They have tolerated my ignorance and allowed me an opportunity to grow.

I first met Uncle Bruce (an author, teacher, farmer and fisherman) seven years ago. He then sent me some of the first murnong, the yam daisy, that he grew and harvested. He asked me to cook them to see what I thought of them from a professional perspective. At Attica we did tests on them in the kitchen and gave him feedback.

Subsequently Uncle Bruce gave us seed, an amazing gift, and we began cultivating murnong in Ripponlea Estate where we grew and harvested produce for the restaurant. This felt special because of the ancient history of murnong growing in this area, although it hadn't been on the land of the estate for around two hundred years. When the bay was a plain, murnong grew across the land in Boon Wurrung country, which is part of the Kulin Nation. It was meaningful growing a food plant that belongs in this area and that has such a long history in Australia.

'I SAW OPENNESS, AND AN INCLUSIVENESS.'

Uncle Bruce and I became mates and collaborated. I think he is one of the greatest Australians ever. I credit him with helping me begin a deep dive into Aboriginal culture in Australia. His legacy will be that he has helped educate Australians about their true ingredients. Because of Bruce I became more and more interested in this culture, not just because it was related to my work but also as a beautiful thing in my life.

It has been a great privilege and honour to be invited to go on country with Uncle Bruce and other Aboriginal elders who I now count as friends. When you're on country with an Aboriginal person, you realise how little you know and how magnificent and beautiful this culture is. Uncle Bruce never has an unkind word to say about anyone, including those who seek to criticise his work or question his identity. His friendship has taught me about the importance of listening, forgiveness and not carrying anger.

My partner Kylie and I are close friends with a cousin of Uncle Bruce's, Uncle Noel Butler, as well as his wife Trish Butler. Uncle Noel is a Budawang/Yuin elder, and the Butlers live in the Burrill Lakes area, on the southern coast of New South Wales. Uncle Noel is a wonderful human and incredibly knowledgeable. He is an expert in Aboriginal cooking and culture, particularly in ingredients from his area.

A few years back, Kylie and I went on country for the first time with Uncle Noel. On the first day Uncle Noel says, 'Ben, we're going to cook some seafood the traditional way tonight. We'll harvest from the coast and pick up some bimbalas.'

I think to myself, *Oh no! Not the bloody bimbalas again! Last time it didn't go so well.*

Four years before, Uncle Bruce had harvested some bimbalas and given them to me. Back then I applied my cheffy cooking knowledge to the bimbalas – you cook shellfish very lightly – and I ate them. They're very high in haemoglobin, bloody and very rich. I thought, *Ugh, these are terrible! I don't like bimbalas, I don't think bimbalas are for me!*

'THERE ARE SO MANY GOOD PEOPLE HERE IN AUSTRALIA.'

That's why I'm thinking, *Bloody bimbalas* as we harvest them with Uncle Noel.

Uncle Noel is using a traditional wood to light the fire, letting it burn down to embers, and grilling the bimbalas. He is cooking them for a long time. I'm not commenting because I have incredible respect for the man and he's far more experienced than me. But I'm thinking, *Oh my god! Uncle Noel, you're destroying the bimbalas!* It goes on for about thirty minutes. I've never seen shellfish grilled for that long before. Then Uncle Noel announces, 'I think they're cooked now.'

The bimbalas look charred on the outside and overcooked on the inside. I eat them and think, *Wow!* They are unbelievably delicious!

I think back to when I cooked the bimbalas in the Attica kitchen and failed epically. Then it clicks: cultural context. I didn't have that knowledge. This was a lesson and also a smackdown. Witnessing Uncle Noel's know-how and his Aboriginal culinary techniques was amazing.

I told Uncle Bruce the bimbala story the other day and he laughed and laughed.

After the last few visits with Uncle Noel, I told him, 'You've changed me forever. I am not the same human because of you. I feel like I can never repay you for what you have given to me.' The mateship of Uncle Noel and Uncle Bruce is a privilege.

ထOOo

'AUSTRALIANS LEAD WITH THEIR HEARTS.'

There are so many good people here in Australia. At Attica, we have a collective who help make the restaurant great. There are 42 employees, more than 2000 suppliers and dozens of 'solid citizens' to influence our restaurant culture.

Almost all of these relationships go far beyond a business transaction. When I get a delivery of the most ethical and beautiful meat from butcher Gary McBean, I'm getting much more than just a product – I'm getting his fourth-generation expertise and his ethics.

Also, I know I can call on Gary for anything and he will come through.

My friend Dave passed away suddenly a few years ago. I was living in the Victorian town of Ocean Grove at the time, and Dave was our unofficial mayor. He had also been very good to my children. The funeral was going to be huge, and I volunteered to make one of his favourite foods for the wake.

Dave really loved sausage rolls so I said to Gary, 'My friend has passed away and I have to make fifteen hundred sausage rolls.' Gary offered to supply not only the sausage meat but also the pastry. My sous chef James and I made the sausage rolls for Dave. Gary never invoiced me for those ingredients. That is a small example of the kind of human Gary McBean is. He has the biggest heart. He's *the* best mate; he's always there.

You just want to be around people like Gary. He offers a great service to his community. It's rare to see somebody of such integrity. He's huge – he's six foot six – and stands in the butcher shop proudly and kindly. It's so beautiful to see the family together working in the shop.

Gary should be celebrated because he is a legendary Australian. As a tribute we created a special lamb pie named after Gary called Gazza's Vegemite Pie and we served it at the restaurant. You don't meet humans like Gary every day. Then again, maybe in Australia you do?

Another supplier who has become a good mate is mussel farmer Lance Wiffen. The first time I met him, I wasn't coping with everything in my life, including working 90 hours a week and not seeing my children enough. I was in a really bad place.

For months it was hard to get out of bed. I hadn't really talked to anybody about it because I grew up with a back-country New Zealand farming mentality where you are stoic.

I'd planned to meet Lance because I was really frustrated with the quality of the mussels that we were getting at Attica. I'd asked the seafood supplier to give us all the mussels on offer. He gave us mussels from five suppliers and Lance's mussels were miles ahead. I organised to meet him at his farm.

Out on Port Phillip Bay in the fresh air, Lance opened up about the hardships he had faced in his work and personal life. There were a lot of connections to my life. It was one of those times where your life goes in a different direction than it could have. Lance helped me through a really hard time. Inspiration can come unexpectedly if you are open to it.

On that day I ate Lance's black mussels, which are native to Port Phillip Bay, and I was inspired. 'These are the best mussels I've ever eaten!' I said. 'Mate, these mussels are incredible! These are absolutely world class, Lance!' Lance had never had that feedback before.

Like Gary, Lance provides a great service to his community. Sometimes when chefs talk about beautiful ingredients, they're talking about ingredients that other people can't access, but these mussels are affordable and available throughout Melbourne. In fact, Lance's phone number is on the mussel packaging so you can call him and tell him you love them!

Attica is a small restaurant that unexpectedly became a global sensation. When this happens, there's a chance that you can become disconnected from what's going on in your direct environment. I've always tried my best to remember where I came from and what it was like to struggle before the privilege of being celebrated and travelling internationally. Before the pandemic I'd grown wary of this life. It just didn't have the meaning that I'd hoped for.

There is a strong sense of community where I live and work. Although some commentators talk about the tribalisation of our society, I've found the opposite to be true.

In March 2020 we turned to takeaway in a desperate attempt to save Attica and the jobs of forty staff. Our community has been with us every step of the difficult way and people stood outside Attica in the rain and the cold waiting to be fed. It's impossible to properly express in words what this means to me. I've shared touching moments beyond what I thought possible.

'AUSTRALIAN MATESHIP IS NOT ONLY ABOUT THE GOOD TIMES'.

On the very first day of our takeaway offering a woman came to our bakeshop to buy a $7 piece of baked cheesecake with the little money she had left from her very last pay. She had lost her job but still wanted to support us. We shared a profoundly humbling moment as we stood, talked and cried.

In the middle of the second Melbourne lockdown a widow wrote to us to say her husband had passed away during the pandemic. Their daily ritual had been to set the table formally with candles, napkins, wine and food, and to sit down together even when he had difficulty eating. Since his passing she had been unable to bring herself to sit down at the table, such was her grief, until she ordered an Attica At Home menu for delivery. She wrote that it inspired her to set the table and sit down like she once did with her husband. Heartbreaking and touching.

In Australia I learned that kindness is much more than being nice or agreeable. It comes from the heart, from a place of confidence and sometimes of forgiveness, and is without ulterior motives. I feel that any time that I need help in this country, people will be there, my friends will be there. Australian mateship is not only about the good times, but also about the hard times and I think that's what the definition of true friendship is.

In our darkest moments our community has been there for us. There is nowhere else I would rather be.

Ben with René Redzepi and Lance Wiffen near Portarlington, Victoria

CHAPTER 7

Kylie Minogue & Kathy Lette

THE FRIENDS YOU MAKE, MAKE YOU

Kylie Minogue and Kathy Lette have been friends for almost 30 years. Kylie is the highest selling female Australian artist of all time and Kathy has now written 17 best selling novels. She is published in 17 languages.

'BENEATH THE BONHOMIE AND BANTER, THERE'S TRUE-BLUE LOYALTY.'

Kathy Lette

Aussie women are each other's human wonder bras – uplifting and ever supportive. Aussie mateship is legendary – Antipodeans are a fiercely loyal breed. But 'mateship' has a blokey connotation and believe me, Aussie female friendships are equally as strong and life-affirming.

My favourite human wonder bra is Kylie Minogue. We've been keeping each other buoyant for almost 30 years. Our (B) cups run-neth over with love.

We met in the '90s at a dinner at the home of another legend-ary Aussie musician, INXS's Michael Hutchence. In the company of such rock and pop star royalty, I was trying my best to act cool, suave and sophisticated . . . But then Michael noticed that my hair was moving. My heart flopped like a pole vaulter into a mattress. I knew immediately what it was – nits! An occupational hazard of motherhood . . . and I'd just hugged the iconic Ms Minogue!

'Oh no! What if I've infested you?' I gasped.

And how did Kylie react to this Dickensian dilemma? She laughed, rolled up her sleeves, pulled on the marigolds and spent the next hour coating my scalp with some thick, foul-smelling goop excavated from the back of the bathroom cupboard. The only way a nit could survive in my hair now was in a flame-retardant wetsuit and an aqualung. I was no longer contagious, but I don't think 'cool, suave and sophisticated' quite covered it.

But Kylie found my slicked-down Al Capone hairstyle hilarious. And we've been laughing together ever since.

Kylie Minogue is rare in the celebrity world, a self-made woman who doesn't worship her creator. She should go through the tunnel of love holding her own hand, but my beautiful bonsai pal does not keep fit by doing step aerobics off her own ego.

Kylie, Kathy and Dannii

Kylie with her brother, Brendan (left) and sister, Dannii (right)
on a family holiday in Queensland

Ours is an unlikely friendship. Kylie is a style icon, while my fashion sense is tongue-in-chic. Worse, my musical talent is non-existent. When I sang karaoke for her once, she asked if I took requests.

'Sure, what would you like me to play?'

'Gee, I dunno . . . Monopoly?' she teased.

Teasing plays a big part in Aussie mateship. In our friendship, it's particularly apparent during our many Scrabble competitions – which she invariably wins. (For Kylie a 'night on the tiles' means beating everybody else on the board. Her name alone is a triple word score.) The Pop Princess regularly takes pity on my mum-like dance manoeuvres (my choreographic repertoire consists of 'The Swim' and 'The Skate'), often pushing back the furniture to teach me a few moves and grooves. Knowing my hatred of housework – my skirting boards have topsoil – Kylie also often does the washing-up after dinner.

'IT'S AN EARTHY EGALITARIANISM THAT'S QUINTESSENTIALLY AUSTRALIAN.'

'No worries, Kath,' she'll say, up to her elbows in soap suds. 'I rather enjoy a sporadic spring cleaning frenzy . . . in winter, summer and autumn too.'

Why? Because even though Ms Minogue's star quality is so great she could have her own galaxy, this is a woman who has both feet planted firmly on the ground. It's an earthy egalitarianism that's quintessentially Australian. Despite being the highest selling female Aussie artist of all time, clocking up sales of over 70 million records worldwide and with a mantlepiece buckling from awards, she retains a girl-next-door demeanour. She is, in short, the diva next door.

'One of the traits I love about you, is your ability to treat everybody the same, from maid to monarch,' I say to her over a cuppa in her kitchen, when we meet to discuss *With Love, From Aus.* 'Even though so many famous people want to befriend you, you've never contracted A-listeria. How important are your friendships?'

'Very! Of course, my sister, Dannii, is my bestie. I'm also still friends with girls I went to school with. And my close girlfriends mean the world to me. However long I've been away, we always just pick up exactly where we left off.'

Kylie is equally unpretentious when it comes to holidays. We all love a resort so exclusive that not even the tide can get in, but humble holidays have never lost their appeal.

'I think this is because we always used to have caravan holidays as kids,' she says, fondly recalling her idyllic childhood camping trips to Phillip Island. 'When we finally got an annexe for the caravan, it was such a big deal!'

I cringe. 'Sorry. I adore spending time with you, but to me, "camping" is what Graham Norton does on his chat show.'

She laughs, adding, 'What about a motel then? I love Aussie motels too. I love the simplicity of them: you drive in, get your key and park your car right outside the front door.'

I prefer the suite smell of success, but there's one leisure pursuit we do agree on – the joy of an Aussie girls' night out. 'Oh, how many times have we had to be hospitalised from hilarity?'

'Yes,' Kylie agrees, 'but beneath the bonhomie and banter, there's true-blue loyalty too.'

'Aussie gals do tend to strip off to our emotional undies, don't we? And it's a psychological striptease that reveals all.'

'Absolutely,' Kylie concurs. 'Aussie female humour is so candid, confessional and deliciously self-deprecating but supportive and positive too.'

Kylie radiates positivity. This is not a woman who thinks 'optimism' is an optical ailment – even while enduring a traumatic medical ordeal in 2005. The announcement that Kylie was postponing her concert tour due to breast cancer sent a tsunami of shock around the world.

'It was a dark and awful place to be.' Kylie's face momentarily takes on a cloudy cast. 'It would get to five o'clock each day and I'd think, *Oh, yes, I got through another day!* It's like a prison sentence.' Topping up our tea, she explains: 'It's like being in an atomic explosion. But it was my girlfriends and family who sustained me. At such a challenging time, "no worries" alone wasn't going to get me through, but that attitude, which is ingrained into the Aussie psyche, certainly helped me cope.'

'When I visited you in Paris, my heart was breaking. Although, even with no hair, you looked beautiful! Actually, you just looked as though you were about to shoot a sci-fi movie with Sigourney Weaver. And we still managed to salvage some humour from the grim situation, didn't we?'

'Yes, it was laugh or cry. Or both at the same time! But it was important to look for the light in what felt like such a dark and uncertain time.'

'Dark? I would have needed night vision goggles. Did laughing at something so serious help to strap a shock absorber to your brain?'

'NO WORRIES' IS THE KEY TO OUR RELAXED, CAREFREE APPROACH TO LIFE.

'Yes,' she admits, raising her famously feline brow. 'Occasionally I went through my really comic phases. I'm like, give me a mic!'

'So, laughter really is the best medicine?'

'Well, it's a great addition. It's really an alternative therapy. Complimentary medicine,' she quips.

To me, this vignette epitomises the upbeat, making-the-best-of-a-bad-situation, can-do, laconic Aussie outlook. I ask Kylie about this typical Antipodean characteristic.

'Oh yes. Even in hard times, there's an ingrained Aussie resilience that nourishes and strengthens you.'

'My grandma called it "cracking hardy". No matter how bad things were – the roof falling in, the river flooding, bush fires on the ridge – she'd give an insouciant shrug and say, "She'll be right. No worries."'

'Yes,' Kylie beams, '"No worries" should be our national motto. It's so much more than just a saying, it's an attitude. In a world plagued with worries, these two small words together exude a casual optimism, even in the midst of hardship. "No worries" is the key to our relaxed, carefree approach to life.'

It's clearly this mix of warmth, wit, generosity of spirit and self-sufficiency which is the secret to her enduring success. (Kylie is the queen of the comeback. Her name means 'boomerang' in the Nyungar Aboriginal language, after all.) Not to underestimate her hard bloody work. We Aussies often portray ourselves as not work, but shirk-aholics

– yet Kylie is the hardest-working woman in showbiz. She's constantly rehearsing, song-writing, recording, touring and performing. I can't believe she doesn't employ a team of people to sleep and eat on her behalf! I suggest that perhaps it's the pioneering spirit which has encouraged Aussie women to be strong, industrious, individualistic and to stand on our own two stilettos?

'Yes. Look at Charlene,' Kylie enthuses, reminiscing about the role in *Neighbours* which proved to be the creative Cape Canaveral that launched her into the fame firmament. 'Charlene was a teenage mechanic, in denim overalls, clutching a spanner. She was capable, independent and making it in a man's world.'

And there's a little bit of Charlene in Kylie still. 'I mean, you've got to be the world's most practical Pop Princess. Because not only do you jump in and do the washing-up, but you're also pretty handy with a power tool.'

I've been backstage with Kylie many times, in many cities and believe me, the Divine Ms M doesn't miss a detail and will roll her sleeves up if needs be.

'Pitching in and helping out is something I learnt from my parents. I was raised to believe that I was mistress of my own destiny and encouraged to find my way in the world. I was blessed with the unconditional support to go and discover who I was and what I wanted from life. And of course, if my dreams didn't work out, I always knew my family was there to fall back on.'

'WHAT AUSSIES DO BEST – CHEER EACH OTHER ON'.

To me, this encapsulates what Aussies do best – cheer each other on.

Australia is often celebrated for the mateship of our Anzac heroes. But it was actually the camaraderie, courage and ingenuity of Aussie women, who won not only the right to vote but also to stand for election in 1902, 20 years before their British sisters, which really put Australia in the global spotlight. At the time, Australia's progressive stance on female emancipation earned us the accolade of most innovative and liberal nation on earth.

And my little mate Kylie continues this sisterly tradition as a sponsor and ambassador for breast cancer charities. Worldwide, doctors have found her advocacy so valuable, they've dubbed it 'The Kylie Effect'.

We decide to have a quick drink before meeting our mates for a girls' night out, where there's little doubt we'll laugh till our lips fall off.

'I think our unwritten Aussie motto is: laugh and the world laughs with you; cry and you get salt in your cab sav,' I suggest.

We cackle like kookaburras, as Kylie swaps our tea for a glass of cabernet sauvignon.

'Because that's the best thing about Australians,' she muses warmly, as we top up our lippy before heading out into the night. 'Yes, we like to wet our whistles, but we also have a sense of humour drier than the Simpson Desert.'

And after this heart-breaking pandemic, have we ever needed a laugh or a disco dance with the Diva Next Door more?

Yep, my dear pal Kylie does not suffer from an irony deficiency. Funny, fabulously talented, fiercely loyal and totally life-affirming, who wouldn't want her as a best mate? But if she beats me at Scrabble once more I bloody well am going to give her nits!

'Growing up in Australia gave me an incredible start – a great education, a desire to travel, experience different cultures and a desire to help the world. We dream big, and hope to live up to those dreams over the years to come.'

Melanie Perkins

CEO and Co-founder, Canva

CHAPTER 8

Kylie Kwong
LIFE–LIFE
BALANCE

*Kylie Kwong is a much-loved and celebrated chef,
restaurateur, author and television presenter,
based in Sydney. She is passionate about food and the
role it plays in nourishing community and culture.*

'FOR ME IT'S MORE ABOUT MEANINGFUL ENGAGEMENT, EVERY SINGLE DAY.'

Kylie Kwong

There is a rooftop I stand on, where I feel completely nourished in every single way. That rooftop, with its beautiful vegetable garden, is a special place that's so cared for by the community.

It's a very loved space, the produce is thriving, it tastes delicious. It's not just an ordinary vegetable garden; it's the Wayside Chapel Rooftop Garden. Wayside Chapel is an iconic Sydney charity that provides essential access to health, welfare, and social services for people experiencing mental illness, homelessness and addiction. As an ambassador for Wayside, I love that the community garden not only provides fresh, organic produce for the meals that they serve at their community cafe, but also horticultural therapy classes for their visitors.

That garden is a place of healing for many of the visitors and provides a connection to community. They go there and literally plant a seed in soil and then watch the seed grow into a plant or food. It's very, very healing for them because they have their own patch of earth. The 'visitors' are homeless people. The garden thrives – it's got worms and composting machines, it's got native ingredients as well as non-native edible plants. And many beehives, including my own.

It means so much that the visitors also tend to my beehive, which produces 80–100 kilos of honey each year. I would buy the honey back from them to use it in Billy Kwong, my restaurant that was in Potts Point. I'd text the Wayside supervisor saying, 'Wendy, I need some more honey for the pork buns. We're making the pork buns tomorrow.'

The Kwongs

The visitors used to proudly wheel my 10-kilogram tubs of honey down from the rooftop garden to Billy Kwong. And I love to remember the pride in the visitors' faces when they knew that the honey they'd been looking after was being used at 'Kylie's restaurant'. That's where it's at for me. Moments like that bring me so much joy.

The pork bun idea was really the essence of what Billy Kwong stood for. It was about local sustainability, it was about delicious produce, it was about celebrating one's Chinese heritage, but also including the community in a compassionate way.

And that illustrates this lovely circle; that life is not always about us, it's about others. How can we benefit not just ourselves but, more importantly, bring benefit to others?

I think it's important that everything we do comes from an authentic and true place. That's why I love going to the Wayside Chapel regularly – to the garden, to the Sunday service, or to sing with the choir. They have been providing unconditional love, care and support for people on and around the streets for over 50 years. These are the people and communities I want to be around, those with integrity and who bring out the best in others.

'I WANT TO USE MY ENERGY IN A DIFFERENT WAY.'

I was 31 years old back in the year 2000 when I opened Billy Kwong's first home in Surry Hills. I've always been pretty manic. Both my parents were like that, my brothers are too. We've always worked really hard.

I'd worked in commercial kitchens and had great mentors but Billy Kwong was my first business, a big learning curve. I did everything in my business, from arranging the flowers to training the staff, hiring the staff, doing the media, cooking at night, helping with the cleaning. My mum did all of the accounts.

I'd leave home at 9 am and I'd just be racing the whole time – then I'd leave the restaurant after midnight and do it all again the next day. It was a manic, highly energetic work environment and I thrived in it. I loved it. Australia gave me great opportunities to make my own way.

Back then I wasn't looking for balance. You know what you're like when you're 31, you're going for it. Fast-forward 19 years and I know I want to use my energy in a different way.

Renowned Danish chef and restaurateur, the visionary René Redzepi, has had a profound influence on how I now think about my work. It's about cooking with a conscience, you know, and how being a chef is about so much more than what you put on the plate. My connection with René has opened my eyes to what a vital role chefs can play in effecting positive social change on a global scale. I see it as a wonderful responsibility. It's also encouraged me to find my truest expression and sense of this country, using native produce, for example.

'I'VE NEVER BEEN ONE TO GO BROADER, I'VE ALWAYS SAID I JUST WANT TO GO DEEPER.'

We had a Billy Kwong market stall at Carriageworks Farmers Market for about seven years from 2010. I loved having the opportunity to work outside in that beautiful environment, and connect with all of my stallholder friends and colleagues who are those wonderful farmers and bread-makers; it's a very inspiring place.

I also curated several large-scale Night Market events there. It was a chance to do something meaningful, relevant, on point, something that I felt passionate about, that speaks to everybody. This made me realise how much I love creative direction and bringing together all my favourite people, food and ideas under one roof.

I used to be obsessed about going to work at Billy Kwong. I would think about every aspect of the restaurant, listening, observing and reflecting, and then thinking about what my message was as a cook, as a restaurateur. I loved the truly authentic and meaningful 'Australian-Cantonese' cuisine my team and I were developing – to me, it was like being able to offer 'Australia on a plate'.

But then I began to feel differently. I started to wake up and say to my wife, Nell, 'I'm feeling a bit like I'm not sure if I want to go in to work today.' Then this kind of feeling stayed with me and I thought to myself, *Okay, that's something you need to look at.*

I felt disgruntled; there was this voice knocking on my door saying, 'Listen to me, you've got changes going on inside of you, I need you to listen to me.' So, I sat up and I listened.

I tend to go where the energy takes me.

I've never been one to go broader, I've always said I just want to go deeper. I've never been interested in creating restaurant chains and empires. I mean, I used to handwrite the specials every night for 19 years – and even when I went away for several weeks, I would write the specials for those weeks and then I'd be texting the staff while I was away, saying, 'These are the nightly specials.' But I know when it's time for change and my mantra is to go deeper rather than broader.

Kylie Kwong with musician, performer and proud Muruwari man, Matthew Doyle

My decision to close Billy Kwong in 2019 was about seeking work–life balance. My newest venture is a casual eatery based in the historic South Eveleigh precinct in Sydney. South Eveleigh was the birthplace of Australia's national rail network in the 19th century, and the Eveleigh Railway Workshops were a source of employment for Aboriginal and Torres Strait Islander peoples and many of these people who travelled into Redfern from the country had family connections here – it really is a very special area rich in history.

At this stage of my career I wish to explore the whole notion of true nourishment. That is, what does nourishment actually mean beyond filling our bodies with good food? There's eating for health and growth and then there's the spiritual and emotional side of nourishment.

I truly believe that when you empty your mind, you create space for new ideas. What I'm doing now is exploring different ideas and communities that I will weave into my new eatery in one form or another. I want to focus on community and collaboration.

My desire to have more meaningful engagement every single day has increased. A lot of it is to do with the fact that Nell and I lost our little baby, Lucky, in 2012. That tragedy taught us very clearly about the preciousness of life. One moment we think we're going to have a baby and everything's gearing up for that moment and then suddenly we hit a big brick wall and our whole life gets turned upside down and inside out.

That was a profound lesson. Every moment is precious, you never know what's going to happen in the next moment. It was a very big lesson about impermanence, that everything changes, nothing remains the same. It's very much shaped the way I do things.

'I'VE REALLY ENJOYED BEING ABLE TO DO SIMPLE NURTURING THINGS.'

I have spent the last 20 years missing out on so many family events, friends' events, all the big events. I was always saying, 'Sorry, I can't come. No, I'm working, I'm working, I'm working.' All restaurateurs go through this.

Nell is so happy now because I can go to all of the events with her. It's really nice to be able to look after her. She is really busy in her art practice so I've enjoyed driving her to 'school' and helping her lug around her art gear. I make lunches for her in the studio. I've really enjoyed being able to do simple nurturing things.

I went up to my mum's the other night and cooked her dinner when usually I would have been working.

These moments are really, really important.

It's been amazing to just stop and slow down. To do nice normal things. Having more time to listen, create, collaborate, engage, read and learn more. That's what I mean by balance.

Elder, Biripi woman Aunty Ali Golding, Kylie Kwong's mum Pauline Kwong,
Elder, Gamilaroi woman Aunty Beryl Van-Oploo

'Growing up in a small Australian beach town, I started out exploring rock pools – but the stars were calling – so now I spend my days helping humankind explore our solar system.'

Dr. Elizabeth Jens

Propulsion and
Systems Engineer,
NASA JPL

CHAPTER 9

Curtis Stone

SAVOUR THE SIMPLE THINGS

Curtis Stone is an acclaimed chef, restaurateur, author, media personality and culinary entrepreneur. He has two award-winning restaurants, Maude and Gwen (named after his grandmothers), in Los Angeles, where he now lives with his wife, Lindsay Price, and their two sons.

'YOU CAN EAT WELL WHEREVER YOU ARE: ON THE WATER, AT THE BEACH, IN THE BUSH AND EVEN THE DESERT.'

Curtis Stone

I can remember hot summer afternoons as a kid walking around the neighbourhood and smelling the sizzle of sausages in the air and thinking, *Someone's having a barbeque . . . I wish I was in there right now.* Because I knew there'd probably be a bunch of people outside, jumping in and out of the swimming pool. And if they didn't have a pool they'd set up a sprinkler so you could sit under it for a minute and cool off.

You don't realise what is unique about Aussie hospitality until you live overseas. What's not often spoken about is the way Australians socialise – we're pretty relaxed, we don't analyse stuff too much here. And we are lovers of the outdoors.

A barbeque doesn't have to be at home, it could be by the side of a river or on the beach – we're pretty innovative.

You don't need to call ahead and get permission to take a friend with you to a barbie, and I think that's unique. If someone turns up with a friend you haven't met, you're never thinking, *Oh my god, I can't believe they showed up with a stranger.* My American-born wife, Lindsay, always laughs about this. She says, 'The Aussies in your life just come over!' They're totally unannounced, not even a call, or 'I'll be there in an hour'. The doorbell rings and sure enough, there's an Aussie standing on the other side of the door.

We are really good at just dropping in and being dropped in on.

While Australians are very laidback and naturally pretty casual, we pay a lot of attention to ingredients and getting them in their best possible circumstances. Fresh, organic, natural – all the important stuff – is pretty high on people's minds in Australia.

The seafood in Australia is exceptional. There's a uniqueness there because of our geographic remoteness. We have things that you don't find everywhere, whether it be Balmain bugs, Moreton Bay bugs, or Australian rock lobster. There are fish that I haven't seen anywhere else . . . such as flathead.

'WE TAKE OUR FOOD VERY SERIOUSLY...'

One of our suppliers at Maude is a Tassie fisherman named Mark Eather. He learnt the ikejime fishing technique, which is a very humane way of treating fish when they're taken out of the water; it also produces the very, very best results for eating. Mark cares about sustainability. He's got a real following from some of Australia's best chefs because he's introduced the concept of 'let me tell you what I'm going to give you', instead of letting them say, 'I'm the restaurateur, I demand I have this fish all the time, whenever I want it.'

At Gwen, our beef suppliers, the Blackmore family, have been running 100 per cent Wagyu, which is a Japanese breed of cow. It's a really interesting moment I think in our culinary history because you've got an Aussie guy in David Blackmore producing Japanese beef in Australia, in my humble opinion as well as anyone in Japan. The Blackmore family's business embodies that 'be creative, work hard and have a go' attitude.

Aussies are particularly proud human beings, so we tend to latch on to these techniques and do them with real pride and vigour, be it producing amazing food, wine, spirits, beer, or coffee!

I often joke and say the coffee in Australia is probably better than the coffee in Italy. I'm sure I'd upset a lot of people if I said that in different parts of Europe, but the truth is we have a real coffee culture and we take it really, really seriously. We've managed to evolve and elevate the way we serve coffee to the point where it's become a real part of our lifestyle.

'Fresh, organic, natural – all the important stuff –
is pretty high on people's minds in Australia.'

If someone said, 'Tell me the Australian national dish,' I'd tell you it's probably spaghetti bolognese. There's nothing Australian about that dish by the way, it literally comes from a city called Bologna. We've just adapted it and we use tomato in our bolognese.

We've begged, borrowed and bartered from different parts of the world when it comes to our cuisine. We are a multicultural society and this has influenced all aspects of our cooking.

You can go to different pockets in major cities and have totally different experiences because of the migrant influence. Take Melbourne, for example. It has the second-largest Greek population outside of Athens, and you can head to Footscray and Richmond for Vietnamese culture and then cross town to Lygon Street in Carlton for real Italian culture and cuisine . . .

We've also got a huge Asian population in Australia so we're home to some really creative, skilled and diverse Asian chefs.

Our immigrants came over here and did the really hard jobs. A lot of those opportunities for immigrants were within the culinary world and still are today. You can walk into a kitchen in Australia and find people from all over the world working there.

Some of the jewels showcased in our cuisine are the result of our 'fair go for everyone' attitude.

There are traces of our convict history in our cuisine. It can be a little anti-authoritarian – chefs are prepared to break rules in the kitchen. It's a Ned Kelly kind of an attitude and it came to life I reckon around 30 years ago in the late '80s. There are still elements of it today.

'WE CAN BE A LITTLE ANTI-AUTHORITARIAN.'

We are very individual and want to do things our own way. Even in how we produce our food and drink.

Aussies have always drunk their fair share of beer and in the last decade, from Western Australia to Queensland, we've really started to think about different ways to brew it. I recently met pro surfer Taj Burrow, who's got his hand in a Margaret River brewery over in Western Australia. They produce a beer named Honest Ale. They literally use ocean water in their beer. When Taj told me this, I stopped, and said, 'Hold on, you're taking the ocean water and . . .'

And Taj is like, 'Yeah, we were using clean water with salt in it, and then we're saying, why wouldn't we use ocean water?' And sure enough, it ended up being one of the ingredients of the beer.

The way Taj is making his beer shows off our innovation as a country, as well as our determination. You can see this attitude in our distilleries as well.

If you go down to the south-eastern part of Tassie, there is the most pure water and this incredible salt air pretty much blowing from Antarctica. There's all of this incredible natural untouched space, rolling green hills, crystal clear water . . . and then when you start adding up all of those elements you can conclude that this is what makes the best whiskies in Scotland possible.

And then you think, *Alright, well, can we make incredible whiskey in Tasmania?*

The answer's been recently proven: yes, we can. It's a very, very new experience. If you'd asked a whiskey drinker 40 years ago what kind of whiskey they make in Australia, they'd have laughed at you – we didn't make any.

If you look at Australian chefs' trajectory, as well as the Aussie winemakers, it probably all started with us looking at each other one day and saying, 'Well, we don't know how to do it,' so the wine-maker went off to work in vineyards in Bordeaux and Burgundy and the chefs all took off and cooked and learnt from European chefs.

We've been doing that for a while in Australia, where we go somewhere else, we're impressed by a product or process, then we bring it home and make it our own.

There are French techniques used in our winemaking but we're now adapting that to be a particular style of Australian wine. It's not just the big shiraz we make in the Barossa Valley. There's a variety of different things that we're doing that are distinctly Australian, from aromatic cabernet sauvignons to really nice chardonnays.

The Hunter Valley and the Yarra Valley also have a diversity that is really splendid. They show we've been able to bring grape varietals from France and Italy and try them out with great success. In Tasmania they're making some sparkling wines; I never thought I'd say it, but they rival great vintages of champagne.

We're constantly finding new things we can be good at.

'AUSTRALIA'S NATURAL LANDSCAPES MAKE TRULY UNIQUE DINING EXPERIENCES.'

The first thing that strikes me about Sydney is its geographic makeup – the whole city is built around this incredible bay and extends out to amazing beaches. With the beautiful views come beautiful restaurants and a real sort of surfy, cool mentality. And the food stands up and matches the surrounds, whether you're talk-ing about local fish and chips or Icebergs at Bondi and Catalina in Rose Bay .

I always tell people that they should go to the country and eat in a pub and have a 'parma and a pot' – that's a parmigiana and a beer. We do have this incredible countryside and country pub cul-ture is very much alive and well.

Australia's natural landscapes make truly unique dining expe-riences. Here, more than anywhere, you can eat well wherever you are: on the water, at the beach, in the bush and even the desert.

Curtis foraging with Paul 'Yoda' Iskov in Margaret River, Western Australia

Brian Lee, Curtis and Brendan 'Bundy' Chaquebor

I recently based the menu at Maude around Western Australia and spent time travelling around exploring the local food and drink. The Margaret River region over there is beautiful; it still feels very, very untouched. Of course it just happens to be where they produce unbelievable waves as well as wines.

'YOU WOULDN'T BELIEVE HOW MANY DELICIOUS AND FRESH INGREDIENTS CAN BE FOUND ON A HUMBLE BEACH'.

I've been foraging in many parts of the world; in Europe, I've been searching for mushrooms in the forests but I had never been foraging in Australia. With the guidance of Paul 'Yoda' Iskov, I went foraging on a Margaret River beach. I walked the foreshore, a place where I would usually go for a surf, and Yoda explained how his inspiration came from the Indigenous Aussies, the First Nation Indigenous women, who showed him the way to source native ingredients.

He had incredible knowledge of green tree ants, native stingless bees, the fauna that is edible and how to get the most out of it. We were wandering, snapping flowers and leaves off different shrubs and plants. You wouldn't believe how many delicious and fresh ingredients can be found on a humble beach.

It's got a real surf culture which is especially Australian and really cool. It's funny, you go to somewhere in the US such as Napa Valley and you're thinking, *OK, it's all so maxed out*. But when you're down in Margaret River you're thinking, *Oh my god, this is just beginning and the potential down here is really vast.*

I also went up to Broome and was guided by two Indigenous men, Bundy and Brian. We did all sorts of things, including what they call fish poisoning. There's no poison involved, but there's a native root that they grind up on a stone, almost like it was a piece of ginger on a grater. They take that and it removes the oxygen from the water, which stuns the fish. It was remarkable to see.

'IT WAS A PRIVILEGE TO EAVESDROP ON ABORIGINAL CULTURE'.

When you're out there in the bush, listening to the First Nation people tell stories, you realise you're very much just a part of a very big incredible ecosystem, learning when the wind changes and when the tide comes in and out and when this flower breaks from this particular tree; that's the time of year that these fish will be running up and down the coast.

Those Dreamtime stories that you hear – they're super spiritual and mythical but they're also saying, 'This is how you're going to get dinner tonight, mate.' You realise this is just a different kind of Australian hospitality, coming from the land.

'Growing up in Australia made me believe anything was possible. The big sky at night and the hope that abounds in the nation's psyche – it pervades everything.'

Dr. Toby Angstmann

Founder,
Underground Spirits,
Obstetrician, Gynaecologist
and Fertility Specialist

GANTHEUME POINT, BROOME, WESTERN AUSTRALIA

'A pretty awesome aspect of this country is being able to hit the road for
a few hours or more and go and explore somewhere new.' – *Mick Fanning*

YARRANGOBILLY CAVES, KOSCIUSZKO NATIONAL PARK, NEW SOUTH WALES

Hidden away in the belly of the Kosciuszko National Park, the Yarrangobilly Caves
are beautiful caverns filled with diverse, colourful stalactites and stalagmites.

ABORIGINAL HERITAGE TOUR, ROYAL BOTANIC GARDEN, NEW SOUTH WALES

'Being exposed to Aboriginal culture at a very young age
was such a blessing.' – *Chris Hemsworth*

SARAH DOLBY, MARUKU ARTS, ULU̱RU-KATA TJU̱TA NATIONAL PARK, NORTHERN TERRITORY

'Aboriginal and Torres Strait Islander people have a direct connection to the land
and the country, and incredible history that goes back thousands and thousands
of years and that's something really fascinating to me.' – *Ben Shewry*

FLORENCE FALLS, LITCHFIELD NATIONAL PARK, NORTHERN TERRITORY

QUENTEN AGIUS, YORKE PENINSULA, SOUTH AUSTRALIA

'It was a privilege to eavesdrop on Aboriginal culture. When you're out there
in the bush, listening to the First Nation people tell stories, you realise you're
very much just a part of a very big incredible ecosystem.' – *Curtis Stone*

TURTLE EGGS, BREMER ISLAND BANUBANU BEACH RETREAT, NORTHERN TERRITORY

Aboriginal culture is one of the oldest living cultures in the world.
Other than its family friendly pristine beaches, Yorke Peninsula carries
rich stories about Aboriginal hunting, fishing and food-gathering.

WOMADELAIDE, SOUTH AUSTRALIA

This festival attracts some of the most respected global musicians, artists and
dancers to showcase their talents. It's a celebration of cultural differences.

CAMELS ON CABLE BEACH, WESTERN AUSTRALIA

In Australia, the furry tour guides love sunsets, sunrises and long walks
on the beach. It's the best way to show off pristine sand and some
of the most scenic coastlines in the country.

MELBOURNE, VICTORIA

'You can go to different pockets in major cities and have totally different experiences because
of the migrant influence. Take Melbourne . . . it has the second-largest Greek population
outside of Athens, and you can head to Footscray and Richmond for Vietnamese culture and
then cross town to Lygon Street in Carlton for real Italian culture and cuisine.' – *Curtis Stone*

LANEWAYS OF MELBOURNE, VICTORIA

You never know what lies around the next corner in Melbourne.
But one thing is certain – you're sure to stumble upon messy but
mesmerising murals and street art plastered over every surface.

THE MILKY WAY, SEEN FROM THE FLINDERS RANGES, SOUTH AUSTRALIA

CATSEYE BEACH, HAMILTON ISLAND, QUEENSLAND

'It's a place to relax. Feel the sand between your toes and get as close
to nature as you can.' – *Chris Hemsworth*

BONDI ICEBERGS POOL, NEW SOUTH WALES

An extension of the iconic Bondi Beach, the pool has been attracting visitors
and keen swimmers for over a century. There's nothing more invigorating
than diving into its refreshing ocean water.

FRASER ISLAND, QUEENSLAND

'The natural beauty of Australia ... Like you're a small part of something
much greater and more powerful than yourself.' – *Adam Hills*

WINEGLASS BAY, TASMANIA

Australians call it like they see it. A mesmerising pocket overflowing
with white sandy beaches, pink granite peaks, secluded bays and
a symphony of Tasmania's most beautiful birdlife.

CHAPTER 10

Terri Irwin

IF YOU'VE GOT IT GOOD, SHARE IT

Terri Irwin is an Australian wildlife conservationist who continues the work of her late husband, Steve Irwin, the Crocodile Hunter. Terri and their children, Bindi and Robert, operate Australia Zoo, the biggest and best wildlife conservation facility in the world. The trio are currently co-stars of the TV show Crikey! It's the Irwins.

'BEING GENEROUS OF SPIRIT REALLY MEANS LOOKING OUTSIDE OF YOUR OWN BUBBLE . . . IT'S SEEING SOMETHING YOU CAN REMEDY AND HELPING IT.'

Terri Irwin

I am extraordinarily lucky to live in Australia and be an Australian because my perspective is very uniquely 'tourist'. Most people have emigrated here with family, or have come here for school, whereas I ventured to Australia simply to experience the country.

Australian wildlife is incredibly unique and like many people who visit Australia, having a wildlife experience was my main motivation to travel here back in 1991.

When I first arrived, I remember meeting someone who was caring for a wombat in their backyard. I had no idea what a wombat was and actually got to go to their house and pick one up to appreciate how big and heavy and remarkable and impressive they are.

Then there's the kindness of people when they found out my mission. As soon as I said, 'I'm really interested in the wildlife,' everyone knew someone who had kangaroos on their golf course or they had parrots that came into the waterhole every afternoon.

I first came for a visit more than 27 years ago and today there's still that generous attitude of 'While you're here why don't you stay for dinner?' or 'Can I give you a ride somewhere?' It is just the incredible kindness that you find with Australians willing to share their backyard with you. I'm proud that the kindness of Australian people and their connectedness with nature hasn't dramatically changed in the time that I've been here.

A young Bindi Irwin enjoys a cuddle with a koala

Remembering The Crocodile Hunter Steve Irwin in his element

What inspired me most about Steve was a conversation we had when we started filming *The Crocodile Hunter*, and we only had it once. He said, 'What do you think we should do when we have money from filming or merchandise or whatever we're doing outside our zoo work? Where should we apply the money?'

We both agreed that we would put everything we made from filming the documentary series and its counterparts back into conservation and Australia Zoo. For four years we barely broke even. It was a running joke at the end of the year to go, 'Well, where do you want to put all of this cash?' Because there was none.

But then we managed to break into the market in America. We wanted to start filming with the Discovery Network and they explained that our style of filming didn't quite mesh. Wildlife documentaries were traditionally 80 per cent animal and 20 per cent presenter. They said, 'You've got this guy in like every shot and that's not fitting our format!' But then they said, 'We have a little network called Animal Planet and it's got about 250,000 subscribers. If you want to try your show on that network, we'll give it a go.' So, we said yes, and 10 years later they were up to 90 million subscribers from 250,000.

This is something I'll admire about Steve forevermore – his personality didn't change with success. He remained that humble, fair dinkum Australian bloke.

We did reinvest everything in Australia Zoo and it went from two acres to nearly 1000 acres. We opened a wildlife hospital, which is now the largest of its kind in the world. You know, it's a $2.5 million-a-year facility to run. We've treated over 100,000 animals since we opened the facility in 2004.

Steve was always true to his word. When it came to generosity, he wasn't a percentage man. He earned an income the way all of us do and everything else went back to protecting wildlife and wild places. Today we employ 60 people in Sumatra just to go out into the forest and dismantle illegal traps and protect the wildlife. These things were so important to Steve. His generosity was phenomenal.

To this day, Wildlife Warriors is run as a charity, so that the overhead is covered by Australia Zoo and 100 per cent of donations go to the charity. So, when you come visit the zoo, you're helping to pay for the administration of the charity. You want to donate to the charity? All your money is going to help this wildlife.

'STEVE'S PASSION WAS PROTECTING ANIMALS WHO DON'T HAVE A VOICE.'

That's thanks to Steve's ethics, the way he was so passionate about protecting animals who don't have a voice and we, the Irwins, will continue that, as long as I have breath.

I think you're really blessed when your kids have that appreciation for the world around them and our incredible wildlife. Bindi and Robert are just amazing. From the time they were quite little, they've had a passion for wildlife and conservation and protecting our beautiful creatures.

When Bindi was little she would even instruct visitors to Australia Zoo to step over the little lines of ants that might be bumbling across the footpath. Robert's passion for crocodiles really showed itself from the time he was about two years old.

That philanthropic spirit and that generosity of nature is something that Australians really showcase. I notice with Bindi and Robert there's a desire to help every living thing and everyone who needs a hand. Robert recently heard about a gentleman who'd suffered an accident and was trying to get a wheelchair that could go on the beach. Robert wanted to do some fundraising, so he donated some of his photography work to a charity auction to try and help Jacko get his beach wheelchair.

It's wonderful, that sense of mateship. That willingness to step up and help someone when times are tough. I don't think anyone does it better than Australians.

'THAT PHILANTHROPIC SPIRIT AND THAT GENEROSITY OF NATURE IS SOMETHING THAT AUSTRALIANS REALLY SHOWCASE.'

Lady Elliot Island is located at the southern end of the Great Barrier Reef and fortunately it has been spared some of the environmental challenges that reefs around the world are facing. We still have a really rich marine biodiversity.

I've been going to Lady Elliot regularly since I arrived in Australia and met Steve. Holidaying there as a family when Bindi and Robert were small was fantastic because one of the other beautiful things about these remote areas in Australia is that they're so safe.

There's a sense that you can let your kids be free range kids, beachcombing and enjoying their environment without constantly hovering over them. Let them make their own discoveries. Part of the discoveries that we still do as a family are those beautiful messages you make with the coral that's washed up on the beach. We write our names and little messages, and leave them for other people.

We've had a stack of fun filming our new show, *Crikey! It's the Irwins*, with Animal Planet there lately. Steve and I had filmed *The Crocodile Hunter* there as well as doing a lot of conservation work.

What's amazing is that the island has been so heavily regenerated. It was originally used for mining bird guano. There was barely even a plant left on the island. Now it has so many trees and multiple species of bird. The tropicbirds nest there. The sea turtles nest there. In the winter the whales pass by, about 50 a day. Currently we are working with the people on the island for a release spot for sea turtles.

It's like the Garden of Eden – you can be near birds and sea turtles and they're not afraid. It's a wealth of riches in this fantastic tapestry of our environment.

The Gash family, the custodians of the Lady Elliot Island Eco Resort, are doing a fantastic job in terms of being leaders of sustainable tourism and conservation. This is what people are looking for now, responsible tourism, be it visiting places like Lady Elliot Island or Australia Zoo or doing one of our expeditions.

We want to go somewhere where we know that the dollars we spend are going to help to protect and preserve these wild places that we enjoy.

Terri with her young children, Bindi and Robert

Through our fundraising endeavours, we're always finding people who are incredibly philanthropic and who have that barn-raising attitude. If there's a storm or a fire everybody comes together to help rebuild.

But I've never seen anything like the kindness shown when Steve passed in September 2006. The outpouring of love really did spirit our family up, we appreciated it no end. No one would've been more shocked than Steve at how compassionate and generous people were with their time and advice. All these years later, people are still asking what they can do to help, how they can step up to keep Steve's dream alive. It's just amazing to me.

Just months before he passed in 2006, we sat down and did a 10-year business plan. Steve had asked me, 'Would you please keep things going should anything happen to me.' To now see that things have grown, gotten bigger and better from our original plan lifts us up. We've taken what he's achieved and run with it; I think he would be astonished.

We're so blessed to have over 1200 animals at the zoo and nearly half a million acres of conservation property. We've got 460 staff, over 100 volunteers and international conservation projects. So, with the day-to-day research work and the running of the business, I was very thankful that Steve and I had sat down and made that business plan. Instead of trying to determine direction without my soulmate and my life and work partner, I was very blessed to have at least that real sense of direction with Australia Zoo.

The three of us feel that Steve is watching over us. But what's truly incredible is the number of people who come to Australia Zoo, not just Australians, but from all over the world, who walk onto the grounds and say, 'It's as if Steve is still here.'

For so many people it's kind of honouring their grief journey as well because all of us who have loved someone will experience grief and we all experience it differently. But when you come here, you can say, wow, here's a family, here's a team of people, here are volunteers, here are hundreds of people who are still honouring Steve's life and legacy. It's really inspiring to know that your loved ones still walk with you and you're not alone. To know that it's going to be okay.

We can affect positive change wherever we are and whatever we're doing. I think we need to look at how we can affect some positive change as travellers, tourists and residents of this beautiful country.

'WE ALL HAVE THE OPPORTUNITY TO LEAVE THE WORLD A LITTLE BIT BETTER THAN WHEN WE GOT HERE.'

When it comes to life, it's all about that idea of really treasuring what you've got and really trying to enlighten others and share those experiences to give everyone those great moments. At the end of every day, we sit down as a family and we share three things. What was your favourite part of the day? What are you most looking forward to tomorrow? What was your good deed today?

I think if we all approach life like that, we're going to make sure that our fellow Australians, our visitors to Australia, and our own mental health just shine. Because we're going to appreciate what we've got, look forward with hope to tomorrow and try to make a little bit of positive change every day for someone else.

AFTERWORD

'WE HAVE AN ATTITUDE TO LIFE THAT'S WORTH BOTTLING.'

Paul Hogan

I am the luckiest man in the world. Back in the 1970s I was a rigger on the Sydney Harbour Bridge. I used to go up there with a 60-pound cable over my shoulder, no harness and it was no big deal. My job as a rigger was to put up all the working platforms and flying foxes and make it as safe as possible for the painters.

I had the best view in the world working on top of the bridge. I would look out at the harbour, out to sea and across the city back to the Blue Mountains. People now fork out money to visit my old workplace. They're chained together in little groups and do the BridgeClimb to get the view and experience the lifestyle that I had every day.

History will tell you I left that job behind after I was discovered on the television show *New Faces*. I wasn't brilliantly funny, but I was very Australian. I never kidded myself. I worked out a phony act as a tap-dancing knife thrower who couldn't tap-dance or throw knives. That was all part of the stir. I went on the show to take the mickey out of the judges. Australians love to stir.

A few years after that I went on to write and create *Crocodile Dundee*. When we were looking around trying to find a director for *Crocodile Dundee*, my mate John Cornell asked Peter Weir, a real world-class director, if he would direct it for us. And Pete said, 'Oh mate, I've got too much on my plate.' He said, 'Do it yourselves, it's not that hard.' So we did.

After the film came out in 1986, the two most famous Australians in America were the golfer Greg Norman, known as the Great White Shark, and Crocodile Dundee. Not a great look for tourism!

They recently did a survey in relation to tourism, and Mick Dundee is still probably the most famous Australian. I'm never on the list, which is great. They don't know my name. But they all know Mick Dundee.

Basically, I had a go – that's been a lifetime thing of mine – and things worked out pretty well. I was a late starter – unlike most people in the entertainment business, I worked in the real world, and I had a proper job until I was 30.

I think Australia is still a lucky country – there's scope, there are opportunities and we have an attitude to life that's worth bottling.

Having spent a lot of time in Hollywood and overseas because of my film career, I reckon what sets us apart as Australians is that we are laidback. That word was invented for Australians.

I'm an old Australian, I'm of convict heritage, all the way back to Vikings and then Irish. My people were thieves and layabouts, so I understand that it is in our nature.

This is a country where people say, 'G'day, how are you going? Come over here, I've got a barbie going.' Like the Australian Tourist Commission TV ad I did in 1984: 'I'll slip an extra shrimp on the barbie for you.' That's what makes Australia a great place to visit – you feel welcome, and you're with people who know how to have a good time.

The thing about Australians is, we're bloody good company. Everyone's got a story to tell.

Our mateship is founded on a 'can I give you a hand' attitude. This is the best country in the world to have your car break down on some out-of-town road. If you're in other countries I've been to, well, good luck. But in Australia, you break down, some boof-head will pull over if he sees the bonnet up, stride over and say, 'What's the problem?' And more than likely fix it, or at least have a go. I love our 'what's up mate?' approach.

'THERE ARE THINGS I DIDN'T REALLY APPRECIATE UNTIL I TRAVELLED OVERSEAS'.

For example, you can just back your car up to the ocean and turn it inland, and from almost any city in a couple of hours you can be in the outback. There's plenty of elbow room out there in the outback. We've got a whole continent.

I remember going to beaches in Europe where you paid to get to the beach, paid for a cabana to change in and you paid for an umbrella. Then you went and sat on the gravelly sand. You were sandwiched between people on the gravel; there were someone else's feet in your face. The water had a few bottles and things floating in it.

I remember thinking, 'Oh, these poor bastards, if only they knew. This is not going to the beach.'

In Australia, there are beaches you can go to and be the only person there, but if you want to go to Bondi and be surrounded by beautiful people, that's all right too. We've got 35,877 kilometres of spectacular coastline . . . and it's not gravelly sand.

The Northern Territory is an amazing place to be, especially when the big wet comes.